NOW

MOLLY TENENBAUM

NOW

·poems·

THE DOROTHY BRUNSMAN POETRY PRIZE

BEAR STAR PRESS

NOW © 2007 by Molly Tenenbaum

10   9   8   7   6   5   4   3   2   1

BEAR STAR PRESS
185 Hollow Oak Dr.
Cohasset, CA 95973
www.bearstarpress.com

Cover art and design by Ellen Ziegler, *www.ellenziegler.com*
Author photo by Tom Collicott, *www.tomcollicott.com*
Book design by Beth Spencer

The publisher would like to thank Dorothy Brunsman
for her generous donation of the prize.

ISBN: 0-9793745-0-2
ISBN: 978-0-9793745-0-0
Library of Congress Control Number: 2007926029

for Ellen

Mother told me when I was a Boy that I must "turn over a new Leaf" – I call that the Foliage Admonition.

– Emily Dickinson, letter to a nephew

CONTENTS

MY NEW LIFE

I'll start it after lunch.

Maybe staring at the mountain
will encourage it,

twinkle of someone's dropped
watch in a crack.

How dewy, washed, transparent all will be then,
how musical, rilling and coursing.

And yet, all along, we were
eating buckwheat pancakes every Sunday.

I'll start at midnight, when the registers
re-set, checker on break.

I'll slip out with eggs in my pocket.

I'll start when the white-with-pink-blush peaches come in,
when the jam has foamed, when every single pot

in the kitchen crusts in the sink,
when there's not one more clean plate.

When the mail arrives, when both hands hit twelve.
Soon as the kettle boils.

After a license plate with an X in it,
a graveyard, and two fields of cows.

Exactly when a color no one's seen before
dabs straight up in the dawn.

When the bourbon rose's cream petals,
worn as old underwear, loosen

at the hip and drop
to the summer-tired grass.

I'LL START IT WHEN THE APRICOT
MAN BRINGS HIS DRY-FARMED FRUIT

It's an old orchard, he says, grown over in oak.

The apricots are tiny, plush,
they are honey, pure custard, sunset condensed.
They are little spoons, they are globes,
they are downy earlobes, orange lights, they are tiger,
they are the bee-drop center of an open flower.

They are the color I look best in, color
I scan the rack for at thrift stores,
color of my favorite summer dress,
scoop-neck, slipping, loose

over breasts plush as apricots, maybe,
and the deer with their delicate hooves
step tender in the leaves, oak heating up
in the sun-dust and sage,
everything softening, sweetening, can't
get riper than this.

I LIVE IN A YELLOW ICE CREAM TRUCK

Red script flourishes, circling itself.
A blue square, one per side, sets off a white swan.

It was the rubber gasket
compressing
that whispered the hither.

I wondered, at first,
was it all one space, or did each door close
on its own small box?

At the back, a pull-down gate.
A little bed, a book, a pair of socks.
The inside walls are quilted tin.

The swan, daubed gray for shadows,
jogs as the truck jogs, over a bump,

and who knows if that counts
as motion – not even the blue
she's painted moving through moves,
her angle depends on the truck, on where

it's going, and under it,
on streets ascending, and under them,
on the whole dark dirt world, a city itself,
of mica and sand, wire and pipe.

I don't believe one world is more real than another.

Remember when they sent people to caves
to see when they would sleep?

One little railing for earrings and a mirror,
and for the night, a wide-mouth jar.

It would be better, I admit, with windows.
At night, hatches latched, it's pitch till morning.

What do I miss? Air.
I love the blanket-stitched sides
and the rumble of warming.

Darling, why am I sad?
There's nothing like a cubby.

Nothing like a pair of boots
and a bed that folds up.

MY PREFERENCES:
A PROFILE FOR PROSPECTIVE LOVERS

Parallelograms and ellipses.
Lines, as in wood grain and sediment, silk and sliced cabbage.
Salt, the crunch and shine.
Shapes moving slowly, especially gray ones.

Cats, mainly, if not for the animate snout
of Billy-the-dog, his spots
like the flecks on my earth-tone teapot.
Black pepper, lots and lots.

To walk, walk, walk, spouting
opinions of gardens – blackberries, yes, dripping down, yes –

To close the curtain at night, but not till the last
pink smudge has rubbed the hips of the vases.

Mustard seeds jumping in ginger-oil,
cascades and tumbles in music,
bow-shakes, damped slides, anything
for texture, long as nothing, but nothing
stops fluid motion –
For language, hand, wood, stone.
Homemade, and that includes dessert.
Corers, pitters, beaded purses,
rusty tools no one remembers.

Cross-sections, captions, frontispieces.
Charts of phrenologic heads.
Cow-maps of chuck, round, and brisket.

Coffee like a science trick: grounds in the middle,
steam through a tube to the top.

To eat while it's hot.

Earlobe and flat plate of sternum.
Ribs, and the heart's Chinese lantern.
Lemon, coriander, clove.

Garlic, and all the bitter greens.
Something to bear down on, something to tender,
something to hold on the tongue, stones
with white windings, stones that look blue underwater.
Brick-red and all the timbres of brown.

And if you've cared to read this far, I should tell you
a felt companion has walked by me always,
opens a gold space wherever I go,
has sung to me since the day I was born –
blue, sometimes, at the edges,
flaring or cooling by whatever
bellows or weather –

I don't understand it either.
Could stare forever at sky needling pine and flapping in maple.

Maybe you're sanding a mahogany table
or looking up in the book that fuss-headed bird
circusing up the pollen in the mahonia.
Did you know, early glass drips to the bottom?

I see you through that, if at all,

but let's eat hot pie
and listen to rain on tin.

I love the fall from a struck string like fire on a rope
and the thumbprint pool at the base of a throat.
That beat, that gulp.

The burlap-balled maple.
The afternoon's nimble and narrowing sun.
The silver slug-lines, rain
running where I'd wanted roses.

Weight from water, curtain from cloud, dough-lumps from dawn.
Blue from pink from purple from tangerine-lavender.

Yesterday's curdling clothes from today's closet floor.
Hip over hip in Half Moon.
The heart, a-twiddle
like locust leaves, to its own true self
or to anyone else's.

The teapot, days my tendons twang.

The burden from bicycling up the hill,
the "or" out of "work."
Please, from the pocket, pennies for bagels and haircuts.

The clock-strike from midnight, the never from noon, the slam
    from the sun.

The lour from the low string, the squeak from the E,
the bowing in "Bonaparte" from the tape, triple-time tumbling
down from the trill, keys and tunings from weather,
hot A from August, soft G from the fern-green of spring.

The frail from the fingers, the music from air, the air
from its muscles like winding wisteria wood.

The happy bacteria, warm, from my farthest-back sinus.
The throb from my orbits, the burn, raging string, from my neck.

Cat-hair from under computer keys.
The year-by-year gray from the kitchen's white wall.
Complaint from my chorus, whine from my tone,
from gall-bladdered, gray-haired decrepitude,
the doctor's explanation: "As we age . . ."

MY EDUCATION

Cried when the homework was outline –
Roman numeral and capital letter.
Cried in long division.

Be fine once I started,
they promised. Were wrong,
it hurt the whole time.

Attended personal clanging
and envy class,
hummingbird hand
and apology class.

In mom's nylon gown,
in dad's cotton pajamas.
In his search for a copper color of roses.

In sizes: large coffee, small cocoa,
wide turns the wheel, slender worries
while glancing up from the maps.

In description: to say what surrounds.
In middles of sentences: blank.
In white sauce, in lemon substitutions.

In rooms: why did I enter?
In the body: return
to the glare on the floor

where I knew,
and stand
until I remember.

Fling a thousand résumés, each with tassels and majorettes,
each with levers, gears, ball bearings.

Boom down the street in my pulsing machine,
let windows crack their sockets.

Say "Nucular" loudly.
From balconies, in glory.

Clack in flamenco, each kick a knife.
A swish for each bill in my belly-dance belt.

Chainsaw a tree, rev steel teeth to grind it, trash the dust.

Walk fast with gold straps on my feet,
converse in plunging velvet, leaning forward,
swear without flinching,
fuck all the way to the top.

Climb on *No Trespassing*, walk on red,
step off the curb, looking straight ahead.

With my Sawzall, my magnum, my orbital action.

For me the devil invents a third choice then he's ash.

Deliberation? Already happened.
Born with momentum.
From day one, my mission: plant radio stations.

Each résumé flashing inserts and buttons,
each with a real mouth that closes and opens.

FROM FIRE, THIS IS MY FIRST
OF SEVEN LIVES IN WATER

I'd thought *to swim* meant to linger, splash toes.
The dog and I played Chase-the-Spray with the hose.
Leaping through sprinklers, a pose and a twirl –
Broke her leg, the neighbor girl.

My paintings were watercolor blots.
My chore, to douse fifty flowerpots.
The hose spilled the patio brick maroon.
I loved that word. *Maroon, maroon.*

At summer camp, last to lower in.
How could they stand it, the shock on belly-skin?
What I really love at lakes? Pilings and docks.
For skinny-dipping, I read and lie on the rocks.

What I've known of pools: plugged ears,
And pounding a tilted head for years.
When it trickles out, it's hot.
Of showers: an ex who would not.

Without, that is, serious debating,
Sympathy, and house-heat to eighty.
Of baths: When it all gets intense,
Relax, they say, with candles and incense –

I wallow, but only in words of it –
Rill and *rillet, guzzle, gullet* –
Don't even care what they mean,
Stillicidious, ultramarine,

Pluvial, limnal, deliquesce.
I've never been in a boat, but took a class.
When I practiced on the rower,
The teacher criticized my hunkered shoulder.

The difference, I joke, is that *jet*sam is black,
As if marsh-talk and all the words for wrack
Don't rip, don't undertow.
Someday my mirror will melt, mercurial flow,

Someone will offer a drink, I'll tip up, slow,
A boat-friend will invite me, *gulp*, and I'll have to go.

A SPLINTER SHOWS YOU ARE LETTING PETTY AND TRIVIAL THINGS UPSET YOU; DENOTES A PRELIMINARY SKETCH OR SCHEME; ORGANIC, OF NO SIGNIFICANCE

So deep, a graze wouldn't wake it, but give
weight and *ow*, the sharp stung. A dot was sunk
where I walk, my tap no step-ball-change, but
all change. Glass, wood, metal? I needed light,
an angle. The needle pulled the callus
white, to cooked-fish threads. Sunday, my only
freedom slipping, and for reading I'm stuck
with zippy fragments, ellipses, snips, when
one Jane- or Charlotte-long novel could soothe
time fritzed out in Epsom all damn soaking day.
Figure this: I never got it out, but
next day, the ghost, next day, not a bit, though
I was afraid to set my foot full in
its print, and kept the beat, limp-drop, step-limp.

FOLIAGE ADMONITION

Around here a little too much true life.
Time to quit the old and start a new life.

In yellow washes, in blue silhouettes,
by oxidized truck hulks, you outgrew life.

I regret it all, but mainly the last
ten years. I shouldn't, but I do rue life.

They pierce it with steel or copper needles
to initiate a cheese's bleu life.

Scissors cut time longer. Paper's music.
It's nothing but a glitter and glue life.

Belly lint, a lipstick print, glint from one
brown eye. Add water, stir. Impromptu life.

Whispering, rustling, greening, yellowing,
busting the waterpipes, this bamboo life.

Incubate your snot-rag in a warm place
overnight. What do you get? Tissue life.

I woke up this morning, backdoor someday,
you don't miss your water in this blue life.

Steam of the fields, far-off clunking of bells.
Molly's next will be a grassy moo-life.

TRANSLATIONS OF THE INVOCATION

Please weather open the stiff
barn door of my chest.

Gray and splinter, fling
wide the wing of my sternum,
romp my willing, willow my streaming,
strip and tinge my beating –

Sugar beet, winter, baby beet, green,
O day, O grace, O sweep
your feathery tip, your tongue and lips

along the stitches of my ribs.

Your fountain, your seeding, your airborne
slips, your tattered skips
along the needles of my ears,
the ribs of my scars.

O fatness, roots, O round and radish, tail of dirt,
O craven leaves, O insides crushing
like popsicles, let your spice
be my head, your white, my heart.

White, my head, spice, my heart.

Keep the check marks on separate,
    uncorrelatable pages.
Make up tasks – "brush black streak
    in throat of iris,"
    and check them, regardless.
Slide the stars, unapplied, side to side
    in the dark of their box.
For every check, a chew of dirt.

For every check, a swish to spit it out.
As the teacher said of exclamation points,
    "Once a year, like birthdays."
Or fever them all over, to defy her.
The claw the cat flexes into the tree's stringy bark,
    the earring's glinty gold post –
    let the check mark be anything, anything else.
So you can't tick when the urge strikes,
    clear the house of pencils completely.

Cut up appliance instruction booklets
    and paste the pieces backward.
    Let all displays flash noon.
Set the alarm for that dusty pearl time
    either twilight or dawn.
Some use kava, but it leads to trouble in the kidney.
Some swear by melatonin, but it makes me dizzy.

Substitute a map of U-pick farms.
Substitute breakfast #1, two eggs and toast.
Trade with a friend: her bank, her bills,
    her groceries, her rice milk

you don't even like. Her appointment,
  her results, her news.
Substitute your favorite palindromes.

Try it without penetration –
  it's hot.
Ask for a history first.
Use protection, and don't
  let the wet get on you.
Always pee immediately after.

MY NEW LIFE COMES WITH

a bearded Doug fir,
a shadowed back fence,
and tree-dusted ivy
in humps over what
might be flaked bricks,
beer bottles, or boards;

comes with earth-wood contact,
with stick, leaf, and sod piles
of previous owners;

since weather blows from the south and needles drift
all year, comes with sweeping the roof
often;

doesn't come with a stiff-bristled broom,

but with Sparky and Spanky, neighbor dogs,
who bark out of love
and can sort from matched syllables
each his own name;

comes with not one
outlet grounded,
and with inspector's notes
Dig out from the wall to twelve inches
lay gravel pull grass
from this stringer don't want it to rot whoever
vented the bathroom
fan to the attic was

well fix that immediately;

and with fog like a bath towel
draping the railing, with junk from the sky
clotting black on the fiberglass awning,
a thug of a vine
that will eat the whole porch
if I don't slash it
now, the flower
not yet seen.

My lips are named Pleat. I can't hear what
my breasts are named, singing in tangerine
rackets of clouds' raring harps. Who is named
I Sleep in a Box My Size? I've been called
Honey, but it was an accident.
Who is named Archer stands side to target,
arms taut to the string. Silence my window
and Bell the air but only when it thinks
of other things. At the counter they'd asked
what kind I wanted so I left. Every wall
a lake of blue paintings, in some pools
a dye of black tea. Winter mornings I touch
the smallest possible light. I'm looking
for one even smaller.

BEACH CABIN

Railroad ties, embedded in their gravel, curve up the coast.

Cliff behind tumbling with rock rose, rugosa,
split oaks aiming down.

Sounds of rushing scoop across the open windows and the door.

Old wood softens and lightens with salt,
the room rests upon stilts.
Foam-lines under erase and cross.

Sand making ripples of itself, the wind
an inch off the ground, sand collecting in cones
at the base of each bundle of beachgrass.

Thick-stemmed angelica, succulent searocket,
purslane rimmed rust-red,

and the mind wants to be those colors,
buff and sage, driftwood gray,
the green that might be brown that might be green,
the beige that darkens closer to the wave.

Brown-blue of the slough's ebbtide mud,
lavender on the clams, tiny as pebbles,
that live there, cloudy islands purpled on their shells.

As the ears want to be smoothed in rolling sound,
oyster shells riffling, clattering, quieting down.

This is no place for the body to live —
shore coursing endlessly, sand scalloping
out from under. Black crashes splinter the posts.

But this is where the mind wants to live,
on a shore of small stones, alongside draped kelp,
near floating spartina,
among the footprints of pipers and plovers,
at evening the gold light
westward on the water.

Spacious boards hear the wind,
the candle-lamp flutters.
All night, soft sand, and the threshold
drifts over.

Under the wire the diamond
Under the dire the air
Under the whir the shush
Under the rough the where

Under the grate the murmur
Under the mirror the stalk
Under the talk the lure
Under the hurry the up

Under the black the grain
Under the figure ground
Under the gray the filter
Under the fall the down

Under the obvious what
Under the so what
Under the what what
Under the whistle what

Under the corners blazing
Under the flare the tong
Under the too the narrow
Under the nerve the prong

Under the pace the pool
Under the peace the going
Under the gourd the stone
Under the one the blowing

Give up matching
    shade to day, silk to lipstick,
mood to cloud to hair
    to who
you are, as if
    you know.
Plain Give up, plain
    Listen, you
are old. The world
    has many tails.
Some sheer, some sighing,
    some bleeding dye, some
flock-dotted, purple-ly flowering.
    Some with half-circles
lapped over liver-shaped blobs,
    some with eyes following,
some with tentacles dimpling,
    puckering.
Some tempting
    bicycle spokes,
some chatty with
    dangling glass beads,
some stitched
    to grip mirrors.
Some silk-screened, dripping with weather.
    The cat won't let go
of the end
    someone hiding forgets
to pull in after.

Started out nose-narrow. Didn't know where
or what it would go or become.
Dipped between rocks. Widened as it went along.

Was quick. Could dart to dab, could retreat
from spines and squirts, from cozy caves –
whoops, those walls are teeth – from coils suddenly

not quiescent. Shimmered like mirrors.
Transparent appendages riffled
from the sides and at various angles.

In the scene as a whole, much spinning and wafting.
Colors banded, pooled. Rapid and slack
finning raised ructions from the bottom.

Primaries overlapped slow orange moons.
Greens and purples exchanged, absorbed,
crossed and recrossed, blipping browns and opals.

In see-through flesh,
the eyes, dark dots.
Thin bones kept the fins up.

With a furrowed gill, a liquid twitch,
all in a sluice,
all in a quiver,

as if seeking –
Half a token?
Le WC? La bibliothèque?

Closing at the hind end too, like every rainbowed side.
A tail, ragged, or a ray,
dragged after, ridging water.

Fronds and stalks kept waving. Colors? Yes, still pouring.
And the one we've been watching?
Plenty of crannies where it could be hiding.

Could have drifted, pulsed, retracted, could have
frayed or leapt. Could be anywhere now,
except in the picture.

I'LL FIND MY NEW LIFE IN SMALL THINGS

When staring turns what's stared at transparent,
I'll whoosh through, reassembling true
on the other side. On the other side

of the white pitcher, I will be perfect
balance of form with purpose.
On the other side of Calliope, smallest of hummingbirds,

I will inhabit high mountains.
Near the single leaf repeatedly
slapping the side of the house, I too

will be green in the drizzle, wet, with serrate edges.
On the other side of the darkling beetle – forewings fusing,
flightless, I'm running, rear in the air –

hey, I look funny. I'd meant wings
to glitter over trees, meant to repose
in the pitcher's cream curve.

Small things, yes, but as a rock lifts
they scramble or burrow, their shell-backs ball up.
Looking won't work. So I'll know

by closing the eyes that underneath
are warehouses, buttresses, arches of room,
airports, railways, skylights of room,

patios, big tops, markets of room,
haywagons, cottages, pastures of room
for the hundred-legged, eight-legged, six-legged,

no-legged, crunch-backed, egg-bellied,
pincer-nosed, no-tongued
creatures to scurry or sleep

as they will.

SONG OF THE BRIDGE TENDER

Where have you been,
Tender, tender?
Watching the cars to their sleep,
Dear one, the cars to their sleep.

How do you know,
Tender, tender?
By the tumbling wheels, dear one,
The rackety tumbling over the water.

What do you see,
Tender, tender?
Steel masts all in a row,
Dear one, gliding, gliding in a gray sky.

Whom do you tell,
Tender, tender?
Tell high windows
On all sides, dear one,
And what is still and near,
And all that murmurs
In my room, ruffling
Over my table, breathing over my chair.

Where do you go,
Tender, tender?
Down the stairs
And shut the seas behind me.
Let the rushing cars be swallowed
And the masts thin out to threads,

Dear one, I leave the room behind
Closed like a shell.

What moment is yours,
Tender, tender?
Mine when I ascend
The stairs, dear one, to dawn,
To floods and veils of light,
To no love nor lack,
To windshield suns
Glittering on all
The sashes where far traffic sings
Cupped and closed around me like a shell.

was the man who, when the opening door
tipped a bell, would set down the broken part
he was holding, wipe his hands on his blue
canvas apron, and step from a back room
to see who had come. He'd lift from their hands
what they'd brought, brush dust off the underside,
check connections, wiggle a loose peg, press –
do they fit? – jagged edges together,
run a hand over their box, their housing,
their cantankerous, kinked-up old favorite.
He'd write their name on a tag, a paper
tag on a white string winding, unwinding,
that twirled as they left, door breezing shut
behind them.   Days later, the very day
named on the slip, they'd jingle the door, work
the crumple from their pockets, almost speak,
but he'd be so quick, they'd see the lumbar-damp
back of his shirt. And he'd reappear, smiling,
See, slapping a chair seat, *that'll stay put*,
or with polished Bakelite gleaming, chrome
warm as cream. Only his shoulders would show
as he hunkered behind, *See, now the knob
clicks right*. Now the yellow light's on, now no
blue flash, but silent trust power is pouring,
no raveled escapes, to just the right place.

They'd leave, pulling the weight to their chests.
Silly, he'd think, after all the trouble
of dropping it off, to take it right back,

but chair legs, china chips, worn cords, sprung wires
drag like wedding cans behind everyone,
might as well admit it, he'd think, and return
their beautiful, burnished, hairfine, oiled, their
own, their very own, waving *So long*, for now.

He'd wipe his hands, new prints smudging the old
on his sawdusty apron, turn as the steel tang
grazed the bell. Had he changed? The leftover
parts on the workbench would blur, shining worms,
coiling turds – the filings jounce his allergies,
who do they think they are, barging in, they
don't know what it's like to be called
every time a goddamn bell rings, what am I,
a cuckoo clock, in, out, in, out – distracted
by cuckoo clocks, their pine-cone gold bobs,
verge escapements, pallets, arbors, pipes.
Safe among the shapes. So much for the sweeping
ups and downs of gods. He'll dodge their big
stomping feet, glue back the pieces they break,
bang his hammer till crescendoing racket
covers him all the way up like stove-heat.

Why isn't he the one bringing a broken
thing to a shop and leaving with a fixed
thing under one arm, hero jaunting off?
He's got a wife and two kids, his favorite
foods are pickles, onions, Hungarian peppers,
horseradish, herring, cheese sliced thin
as yellow glass, and he will die soon

of poisons in diet soda, of love
for crocus cloth, tack cloth, emery paper,
Titebond, Tru-Seal, epoxy, Slip-free
Elastomeric Patching and Caulking Compound;
for cracks, as in Great-Aunt Eve's pitcher
he fixed before I was born, and my mom
tells it as a miracle, Eve finding it,
whole, at breakfast, Christmas day; of love
for the woodblock he gave me to pound
nails next to him as he worked – I smashed
each one crooked but that was my real
self pouring through the hammer, sideways;
of love for the butter he wasn't allowed;
and even for those he waves goodbye to,
who tramp off, plug ends flapping, good luck
to them, poor saps, as he turns back
through the doorway, evening a powdery
gray-gold as his outline dims, and he's no
longer a burper, farter, snorer
(now we know he had apnea, never slept
one full night), but a figure intent
on intricate parts, someone lost
in fitting them together, a plump man
in glasses waving before burrowing
down to the clamp, solder, dust, pot, glue.

I WORK AT THE WONDER BREAD FACTORY

High over hospitals and a college,
red sign glowing, exhaling, repeating,
white steam spinning up,
the hill a pink cloud.
Smoke machines couldn't invent this.
At dusk I ascend, I park, I enter the doors.

I'd wear a watch, but the strap would catch.
I wear earmuffs to soften the clack.
I wear white, and on my break, walk out in the frost.
The building is cracked in fine hairs, and my breath
is light like my sleeves.
I'm not cold.

At midnight the trucks sigh, an inch
to spare from the walls.
If a car wants to get through, if a car
wants to pass to the intersection and the light,
just then the street blocks with backing and beeping,
with someone perched up behind glass
pulling hard on a wheel.

I work inside cobbled and green-glowing windows.
I never see flour.
All night, a dusty grill splits light
into pink petals over the door.

Did I plan to cover my hair
with a net and a cotton bandana?
Did my mother, kissing my three-creased knees,

say *Little lapkin, little suckling,*
you will work for Wonder?

I eat whole wheat
and so does everyone I know.

Who has sifted this film on the city,
made the pink clouds, yeasted the fog,
blown what blooms like bread
through the air, while the bread itself
is nowhere to be seen?

Rosy steam lounges, lazy as summer.
Through the clouds, through the fog,
I descend, and once home, I fall –

it puffs up around me, my white bed.

Nicks sticks
un-gums gongs
meters water
winds wands

hammers hairsprings
prinks plates
rings repeaters
evens weights

tempers the ting tang
jingles the stopper
flips the fly-back
re-silvers the chapter

counting down
the circular error
polishes pendula
pins planetaria

quiets escapements
resists recoil
keeps a dead beat
among luminized dials

Recommends a broadside for my butt,
potboiler for my pudendum,
breviary for my year,
chapbook for my lips,
gazette for my eyes,
opus for my corpus colossum,
concordance for my gripes.
For my every move, an engraved companion.

Shows up in time for fall cleanup, says,
why don't I read mushrooms?

Home from a hard day, and there she is, big desk
barricading my door, placard claiming "Information."

Dares me to ask a question.

Sunday morning, earthquaking plaster,
escape to the sidewalk – it's her –
my house her table, her giantess elbows
thunking my roof like bad manners.

What a cadastropher, grouping the maple
with flute, with smoke, with stutter and flame.

Her keywords for "throat": sluice, aquaduct, plug swelled shut.
Likes it that no one else can look things up.

Could, if I knew author from person.
The words for the breath of this moment,
for swifts at my honeycomb silo,

for sweets of my cornucopia pudding
already here, in reversed
spines and anti-betical tumbles
of the returns on the trestle
even now wheeling aisle to aisle.

WE USED TO RUN OLD WORLD FUDGE

We used to run Old World Fudge
down in the market. There was a window
where we sold thirty kinds – Coffee Nudge,
Vanilla Ripple, Macadamia Fool.

Down in the market, there was a window
to our vats, so the tourists could pick
Paragon Praline, Raspberry Jewel
to swing along home, matching and mixing,

our vats tilted, their purses pitching.
We did not make pistachio,
we had to say, matching and mixing
to the hiss of a sugar-jammed radio.

Were sorry not to make pistachio.
We stirred as it cooled,
tuning the itchy radio,
paddling fudge flat on the marble.

If you don't stir as it cools,
iron bars to stop the oozy edges,
if you don't paddle it flat on the marble,
it'll glue your teeth like burnt molasses.

Behind iron bars, always on oozy edge,
we stirred until the sheen dulled,
aiming for tenderness, hands like molasses,
the stirring our private pastoral

until the sheen dulled.
Some makers skip the next step and are done,
but we patted our browns and pastels
into handmade wood molds.

Lazy makers, splat, they're done,
but we wanted clean shapes, something nicer,
our buttery hands lifting the molds,
cutting cooled fudge into squares.

Wanted clean shapes, something nicer,
but I tell you, retail nearly killed us,
cut cold into squares,
the little take-out hatch, grim business.

I tell you, retail nearly killed us.
We used to run Old World Fudge,
hatch of passing faces, our flavors,
Nut Ripple, Divinity Drudge.

The only job is
shifts from place
to place.

Ground to bushel,
board to pot
to plate.

In the bank,
in writing on a check,
in tax.

Body biked over the ridge to work
to speak
to people, and they speak back.

Eyes from full frame
to squint, glare
from bright to black.

The heart, a blanketed
shape, rolls over
in sleep, and a cup

dries on
a different drainboard
the next week.

Plate to scraping, peel
to bucket, to heap,
the layers green-brown,

green-brown, bin-ribs
open in front
for the rake.

SCISSORS SIGNIFY SEPARATION; OPENING; DECISIVENESS, FIRMNESS; MAKING THINGS THE RIGHT SHAPE AND FITTING THEM TOGETHER

When I stopped for a lemon scone and more
scalded milk coffee, the gal was twirling
shelf to shelf – "Where did I put my scissors!" –
to slit a fresh freeze-dried pound. Last night
I found my scissors, the ones that in daylight
stay lost, my favorite pink-handled snips
for basil chiffonade, for lovage, string,
for blue bands binding broccoli. I dreamed
I found them in a box like a microphone
case, foam bedding for a close protective
fit, a box with an extra triangular
unexplained well where no scissor part went.
Without the gal twirling, I wouldn't have
glimmered the dream, and without the dream's
evidence, I'd have been sure I'd jittered
unsleeping all night, skin tight to pin in
the squirming, milk foaming now like
a baby's raspberry lullaby lips, and me
ringing down to the jar – my change, her tip.

APTITUDE TEST

Which activity would you prefer?
a. Sitting with a sick friend.
b. Climbing a mountain.
c. Reading a book.
d. Reading a book about mountains
    to a sick friend.
– Educational Testing Service, from memory

Now that you're settled in the arm
of this desk, do you incline
to watch the pine in all weathers,
the distracting sun on sequins of snowmelt,
or do you seek inside weather a central
shape of tree?

Perhaps instead you wonder
why snow sticks to grass before sidewalks, why lawns
seem like sheets tucked in, borders neat
as the imagined orderly world.

Where do you stand on birdseed,
tons sold every year,
the junco hungry in the yard?

Do you like winter?

Speaking of carpentry, are you for
hammers or nails?

If you had one hour left,
would you fix the screen door handle,

kiss your love goodbye,
or eat at last the habañero,
hottest pepper you know?

Suppose someone offered you,
in the middle of life,
a tray of cucumber slices,
a doily of cunningly cut canapés,
and a third hand brought
rich chocolates, each one in a gilt-foil cup –

quick, what calls,
the shine, the sweet, the strange third hand,
or beautiful cucumber's palest green?

Do you like spring?

Quick, what was your first thought when you were born?

IN MY NEW LIFE I'LL LIVE AT LE PICHET,

where every morning we drink sharp coffee
from heavy white cups,
where, on heavy white plates, croissants,
small and salty, magically
vanish and then there are crumbs.
The newspaper leaves the building
with butter on the inside pages –
I do not follow.

For le déjeuner I choose
la charcuterie, les fromages,
le selection du jour, and for le diner

every night I'll try one more
specialité de la maison, suffering

from all I don't order,
noisettes d'agneau with chestnuts,
compotier de boeuf with pickled eggs, beets,
and radishes, here served in halves,
a sliver of green stem left on.

In my new life, I'll take forever
with the wine list. I'll have another.

Of les desserts, whatever I dream
of all they offer, lemon, chocolate, some red fruit.
No bedtime, so I can have coffee after.

I, with my companions,
will hog the table, even though
others are waiting, though others
come in from the cold
and stand, steaming the entry.

Don't you hate that, walking in
to no table free, but a party of friends
has been laughing for hours –
a wave at the waitress,
a tap on their glasses, more is poured,
they're going to linger, show no sign
of ever leaving, are more at home here
than you'll ever be anywhere?

MY PERSONAL PEACE MARCH

My personal peace march mistypes
"peach" for "peace" every time.
And because, war or peace, I will always
be this kind of person, I have forgotten
to bring the right candle, though everyone
else has put theirs in a jar or provided
paper shields. I'm grumpy and it's my march,
so no "We Shall Overcome," no folky
strummed banjo. No one can make me
grasp the hands of strangers. "I've had it

with lack of erections," says a woman
to her neighbor. That thin man thinks
of home and hot dinner. That woman there
stands next to the man she loves,
but he doesn't know, he's wishing
tomorrow's chiropractic appointment
could fix today's kinked neck. Over there,
that woman is solitary at the edges.
And who's that with the chalky blue face?

That's the spirit of Art, here with a head of clouds.
Also present: the elephant god, the orange god,
the god of blueberry pancakes;
the god of goatskin bagpipes, god of arctic ice cores,
god of the lost Alexandrian library, god
of hot pink fingernails and of dogs
wagging so hard they whip their backs, sniffing crotches.

Watching from under a rock is one of those hearth-snakes
who sips milk from a saucer and who
in return keeps mice from the house.

Here come the ten-year-olds on bicycles,
and the solstice streakers with their cute butts.
Here anniversaries reunite:
paper, cotton, leather, linen.
They race up to each other breathlessly, buss cheeks,
and are wearing peach-colored pantsuits.

At my personal peace march, we watch the gliding,
lighted ferries on the dark water, and the sky,
grayer, more murky than water.
We are gathered by a pedestal
where votives have blown out but glow,
and where, up high, a model of Liberty waves at the boats.
We're in a park full of things we put here –
hamburgers, trash cans, bathrooms.
And things we didn't – night, salt, the tin-flat moon.
We love each other and don't want to say
    goodbye to this world.

YEAR OF THE MYRIAD FRENCH BAKERIES

It ought to have been later already,
but it was still ten in the morning,
ten-thirty, everyone at tippy round tables,
crumb-gunked plates, everyone reading
the movie section, the personals, no one getting up to go.

We were happy to stare at the raspberry,
chocolate, lemon silk tarts,
counting weekends in a year,
chances to try every one.

One woman got a boyfriend
so they could order two and trade halves.

Dawn was crystallized violet, berry preserves,
butter-spot windows on white paper bags.
It opened like a rose,
the petals, butter, apricot glaze
on the frangipane hills.

Almond grit stuck to everyone's shoes.

We rattled Real Estate and Living.
After each sip, set our cups
in the same pools in the same saucers.

We were always stopping off
on the way to work, soft shapes
filling with air, butter scent cloudy in everyone's hair,
golden invisible lines wending up from the doors;

not clear if we got there, the whole solar system
in some sort of cinnamon twist, that orange-shot orb
rising daily, time looking back, longing,
the closer it slowed to noon.
We wanted – you know, those flaky buns
with the chocolate inside, bittersweet dabs,
how do you
pronounce them?

"One of those," we'd say, driving all over
to find the best, and we did, salty outside,
grainy inside, curled like sleeping doves.

If they handed us something else,
tipped like a top hat, honey-glazed,
wing-shaped, powdery-white,

we'd accept it.
Unwind the coils,
sugared nuts dropping,
prise the layers, pull the soft
inside away from the crust.
We'd find a whole pear, sometimes.
We'd unwrap lemon-flecked air.

THE DAY AFTER THANKSGIVING

The soil's just right for weeding,
    not plopping wet, not cracking dry.
You're it My turn You cheated wave the voices
    down the block, *Come home now, come,*
calls Hendrik's mom. *But Jessica's mom says*
    I can stay. Margaret's van hums up,
rumbles away. I know already I won't
    get every root the last owners left,
and where my foot sinks the fork, my arch
    will bruise, levering iron over and over.

And while I discover, tight on the twig,
    like six-pack plastic on the necks of seals,
the label for lilac 'William Marshall,'
    and while I plan to let him bloom
one spring before I maybe junk him – since a lilac by my ethic
    must be petticoatedly, gallivantingly fragrant,
and that great-aunt, faded-apron shade of blue,
    and while I'm thinking, though it's not thinking,
it's shaking dirt through rubber-gloved fingers, it's tossing
    knots of crispy white roots
and grass hanks the color of sand,

    the kids are leaping on and off the rail.
Railing's audience, driveway's stage,
    and the kids fly to center, twirl,
exit, continuously
    making up rules, and making them up again

more elaborately. I'm pruning too much
    Heavenly Bamboo but want to see
the shape and have to keep cutting.

    Margaret's van gravels back, shudders down,
and if the day so far is to know by, evening
    will have Hendrik contriving a hog-wild machine
of buzzers, whizzers, musical bulbs,
    while Margaret, performer of Macedonian dances,
stitches in black and red wool the motif of nine flowers,
    and if apocalypse holds off, if the president
will just shut up, the day after the day after
    Thanksgiving can start where today
never stopped. *See you tomorrow*, we say.
    Come by for leftovers, and hang up the phone,
tripping on wool-balls all the way.

    One year, early snow cracked the yew. One year,
ice crashed the power so we couldn't cook.
    Usually, rain's been slapping for months by now:
these weeds would never pull out of that muck.
    Today, like yesterday, as the report predicts
for tomorrow, is the color California Beach,
    only colder. Last night, my friend's beautiful daughter,
a senior, next year to Art in New York, had her last
    holiday home. Up the street,
Trevor and Heather, hell on bikes,
    who knows what they'll be. Jessica, eleven,
will win MIT prizes, if prizes, if MIT,
    and twelve-year-old Hendrik, knock on wood,

already he builds engines, unfreezes computers,
    hates TV, loves mud, birds, water,
and getting in trouble for dirt.

    I'd better not, in my soon-to-be garden,
plant roots wanting water, better not trust
    Sunset's climate zones, even the latest revised edition,
though I've ordered beautyberry 'Profusion'
    and a creamy aster. Don't want this afternoon to end,
but can't work one bed forever, besides, my arm hurts
    and I need it, since what am I
made for but music, for wood
    carved and varnished, for strings so tight
they can snap an eye out, and despite
    brick-bat brain and hands like walrus flaps,
for touching a finger to wire,

    for in my own version, we evolve by whoever
bowed from blurry gut the first clear note,
    whoever drew an almost perfect
circle with a brush, whoever gazed at a star,
    thinking, for no known reason, "Dog,"
whoever brought an easel to the morgue,
    whoever painted crowd scenes, couldn't bear
the edge of the canvas, kept cramming in
    one more tryst or deception, whoever filled
a band around the bottom of a shift and the sleeves
    with embroidered bouquets, whoever's divinity
came out fluffiest, biscuits the lightest,
    whoever added thumbpick and autoharp

to "You Are My Flower," whoever found
　　that green wood makes a tight chair,
whoever stacked mineral combinations
　　in a can, attached a wick, stood back
for the boom and purple fountain,
　　whoever sewed velour hats in burgundy, aubergine, mauve,
whoever illuminated initials, wound vines, hid animal
　　spirits behind the bar of the *A*, the hatch of the *T*,
whoever could calligraph a hundred characters
　　every day and throw them all out every day,
all for one good one, whoever could speak in prayer,
　　whichever back-porch curmudgeon
whittled the bumpiest fiddle tune,
　　even if no one ever heard it, whichever irked
mapmaker devised a cauldron of circles,
　　whichever socially inept unmarried tinkerer
built exact models of ships
　　from wood and metal scraps
and put lights and people inside
　　and built an ark too, but with no lights or people –

I'd better stop digging, better not torque my wrist
　　that needs rubs and rest – but I stay out
till I'm cold in my sweater, and Heather, Trevor,
　　Jessica, Hendrik, are all called for supper.
Not that I don't want afternoon to end,
　　but depend on the hours in turn,
time in its usual shaded gradations, evening
　　and a potluck dish
to go in and cut potatoes for.

CV

I am the only person on earth
at this moment with a hickey on her tongue.
Wetness like nobody's business.
Whatever it is, it's in the center, churning.

My shape: an ice-knuckled tree.
My glasses: cracked in a necking event.
Solid my best bread.

As for time, I knew names
of every dead fiddler, tune title, hometown, date of recording.
Can learn new things, such as deepening.
Lie on a couch tossing popcorn and reading.

I repeat, with pleasure.
Think in blue.
Fog and brightly.
Was there, I saw
twinkles breathing.

Surge and sand and sorry
to say, my mother too.
I slide paper under spiders.

Goals? To be brave
with inversions, too sour
for infections, the flushed
pinpoint star on my darling's cheek,
entered while watching his face.
To melt and drink.

POEM ALMOST ALL ABOVE THE NECK

The kiss was so amazed at your simmery skin
and your eyes crinkling open that it didn't know
how to take you all in, but made itself up,
a slap-skinny tadpole swimming along
your sternocleidomastoid to the dipperful
of shade behind your hair. But every peach and pouch
was too much; at every cup
it had to pause, part, inspire –
a hundredth of an inch
above the pea-vine of your freckle,
the meringue of your under-eye,
the windfall of your lashes.

It puttered, old butler, straightening silver.
Patted as it preambled.
Laved a line on your clavicle. Rolled as a marble
where you are ticklish, but you let the tickle travel,
let it gaze gold chirps and whistles all over you,

and seeing you could stand it, the kiss
licked the helix, swirled the anti-helix, wished
its air into the intertragic notch, and lolled for a while
in every *L* it could think of –
willow, bundle, hula,
Quetzalcoatl, Haleakalā –
at your earhole's riviera.

Sorrow of cold stoves, of absent trees –
so the kiss grieved each time it left bare

any part of you, trading the chocolate-chip-cookie warm air
of your lobe for your windswept cheek,

sad to have no caper butter or jump rope rhyme,
no echolocation or estuary
to kiss you with; sad it could not kiss
you whole at once, though if it did,
it would miss your jasmine stars
opening as its dewdrop inched, your lemon verbena
uncreasing as its high noon held.

And whether you liquified toward it or not,
believed it or not, the kiss, though how could you not,
continued, its cowlicks of breath,
its fine-tipped brush – if only it could
elongate every cell, tell every follicle,
still all the cilia in the world,
take a stretched-out forever, rowing, rowing –

In the afterworld you'll be able to tell them:
you'd become stars and loosened strands,
you'd been the moon's curve under clouds;
had anyone asked for a wish, right then,
you'd have been able to grant it –

And when it hovered, inhaled, finally
scooped up the distance, your lips disappeared,
warm foam marsala dessert, every taste,
they weren't kidding, almond, honey,

chocolate, basmati, cinnamon, spring, pure
spanking water, buckets of new-dug clay.

And there the kiss wanted to cry for the colors
now too close to see, for your isthmus, your casbah
cushions receding, your arches, palatial and glossal;

for all it could not say, being a kiss,
and far from understanding itself;
but crying was not dissolving enough,
not melted nor orange enough to tell you.

TO ALL MY NEW LIVES SO FAR

1.

You cupped me like a palm of water
   in a hundred-year-old former dorm
for Ladies College teachers, past the hall's last
   lightbulb socket. You dinged me under
a rickety landlady high in a tree picking apples.
   In you, hoisted half up,
I looked through a goldenchain tree
   with squirrels.

2.

You rushed me bare into another
   upstairs apartment too,
though downstairs was basement and therefore
   the upstairs was ground.

3.

In a boggy backyard, you unfurled rhubarb's red babies.
In three of you my throat closed up.
In none of you did I sail a boat or hike to the top.
In you never once was I sporty on teams or in bathing suits.

4.

All I ever did in any of you was hang around Portland in G,
though whiskied, late, we'd crank it to A.
In your chuff and roar, I boom-chucked back-up
faster than I could, and you lasted forever, all the way
to the end of *Let Me Fall*.

5.

Nobody told me I was the only one not on mushrooms.

6.

If I could restart you, I'd be there the day
Rob brought a joint to school, but wasn't, and woke up
at the Renaissance Faire, tooting a recorder.

Wouldn't miss the day in second grade
you introduced Geography either.
Was present for dots and commas – now long
for the looping I knew before pauses.

7.

In your single-stem plum-blossom vase
　　I did not marry or keep over nine years.
In the mirror of your myrtlewood bowl,
　　I did not prune a pear
like my friends in Santa Cruz in the seventies –
　　miserable all along, it turns out – but what
did I know, craving your kick
　　in their kitchen to make me someone
already herself, cranking pan-roasted beans
　　into the grinder's tiny drawer.

8.

I did what I could to delay you,
　　stopping for milk, always waiting
　　　　for full rolling boil. Given a sticky bun in a bag,

I'd save it for home
　　and a rose-painted plate.
　　　　Your blasts blew the doors, your drive-by bass

parked in front. I hid in my ears
    under tongues and buckles, your cannonball decibels
    swarming the linings –

all I could do for quiet
    was dream in black velvet.
      All I could do was die, but still you pounded.

TO MY NEW LIFE

I've been in you
awhile now so
maybe you're not new

or new as each moment
ho hum ta-da
is always new

I've tumbled in storms
of impending you
flamed in flushes

afraid of you all
of a sudden nostalgic for you
the squirrel-tree window

where first I knew you
no cell the same
as any seven years ago

so maybe I never
completely
became you

though I did
feel all new
about two years ago

in the green dress with white dots

My real new life shows through
the life I'm in, blushing
off-orange or tingling after
the fork that fell. Nothing I've said
of it so far is right, but it will be creamy,
like unsalted butter, it will know
everything, even
how to stay crisp on the bottom,
how to be cut
without fruit sliding out,
will be pie itself, berries
bubbling their blue gluey mouths,
gold edges dissolving,
and slow
like the sun wants to be
but can't, poor sun, who would gaze
at the man doing dishes,
the woman quiet and reading,
would pause in the side yards
between the houses,
happy and sad in every color.

ACKNOWLEDGMENTS

The author is grateful to the journals where these poems, sometimes in other versions, first appeared:

Barrow Street: "Things I Can't Lift"
Beloit Poetry Journal: "What My Father Wanted To Be, He Used To Say"
Cider Press Review: "My Personal Peace March"
Crab Orchard Review: "Year of the Myriad French Bakeries"
Cranky: "Translations of the Invocation," "The House Named Imbue"
The Diagram: "I Live in a Yellow Ice Cream Truck," "Preferences: A Profile for Prospective Lovers," "From Fire, This Is My First of Seven Lives in Water," "Solutions to the Checklist Problem"
The Mississippi Review: "To My New Life"
New England Review: "My New Life"
Nimrod: "Beach Cabin"
Poetry Northwest: "Song of the Bridge Tender," "Aptitude Test," "I Work at the Wonder Bread Factory"

The following poems appeared in the chapbook *Old Voile* (New Michigan Press, 2004): "My New Life," "I Live in a Yellow Ice Cream Truck," "I'll Start It When the Apricot Man Brings His Dry-Farmed Fruit," "Because I Didn't in This, in My Next I Will Have To," "From Fire, This Is My First of Seven Lives in Water," "Foliage Admonition," "Lessons of the Nth Lost Scarf," "I'll Find My New Life in Small Things," "In My New Life, I'll Live at Le Pichet," "CV," "To All My New Lives So Far," "To My New Life," "Yet Another Sun Is Always at Work."

"Preferences: A Profile for Prospective Lovers" and "Solutions to the Checklist Problem" appeared in *Diagram: The Second Print Anthology* (Del Sol Press, 2006).

"My New Life" and "To My New Life" were featured on *Poetry Daily* (www.poems.com).

ABOUT THE AUTHOR

Molly Tenenbaum lives in Seattle, Washington, where she teaches creative writing at North Seattle Community College and plays traditional string band music. She is the author of *By a Thread* (Van West & Co., 2000), and of the chapbooks *Blue Willow* (Floating Bridge Press, 1998), *Old Voile* (New Michigan Press, 2004), and *Story* (Cash Machine, 2005). Her CD of old-time banjo is *Instead of a Pony*, and she plays with the string bands Dram County and The Queen City Bulldogs.

ABOUT THE BOOK

Now was digitally set in Century Schoolbook using Adobe InDesign CS. Leaf ornament by Ellen Ziegler.